THIS BOOK BELONGS TO:

D0256251

WRITE YOUR NAME IN

WRITE YOUR NAME ILLEGIBLY.

WRITE YOUR NAME IN TINY LETTERS.

WRITE YOUR NAME BACKWARD.

WRITE YOUR NAME VERY FAINTLY.

WRITE YOUR NAME USING LARGE LETTERS.

ADDRESS

PHONE NUMBER

* NOTE: IF FOUND, FLIP TO A PAGE
RANDOMLY, FOLLOW THE INSTRUCTIONS,
THEN RETURN.

WRECK THIS JOURNAL EVERYWHERE

TO CREATE IS TO DESTROY

BY KERI SMITH

A PENGUIN BOOK

PENGUIN BOOKS

UK | USA | CANADA | IRELAND | AUSTRALIA
INDIA | NEW ZEALAND | SOUTH AFRICA

PENGUIN BOOKS IS PART OF THE PENGUIN RANDOM HOUSE GROUP OF COMPANIES
WHOSE ADDRESSES CAN BE FOUND AT GLOBAL.PENGUINRANDOMHOUSE.COM.

FIRST PUBLISHED IN THE UNITED STATES OF AMERICA BY PERIGEE BOOKS,
AN IMPRINT OF PENGUIN BOOKS (USA) LLC 2014
FIRST PUBLISHED IN GREAT BRITAIN BY PENGUIN BOOKS 2014
016

PORTIONS OF THIS BOOK PREVIOUSLY APPEARED IN THE EXPANDED EDITION OF
WRECK THIS JOURNAL BY KERI SMITH, PUBLISHED BY PENGUIN IN 2013

ART AND DESIGN BY KERI SMITH

THE MORAL RIGHT OF THE AUTHOR HAS BEEN ASSERTED

PRINTED IN GERMANY BY GGP MEDIA GMBH, POESSNECK

ISBN: 978-1-846-14858-3

www.greenpenguin.co.uk

Penguin Random House is committed to a
sustainable future for our business, our readers
and our planet. This book is made from Forest
Stewardship Council® certified paper.

WARNING: DURING THE PROCESS OF THIS BOOK YOU WILL GET DIRTY. YOU MAY FIND YOURSELF COVERED IN PAINT, OR ANY OTHER NUMBER OF FOREIGN SUBSTANCES. YOU WILL GET WET. YOU MAY BE ASKED TO DO THINGS YOU QUESTION. YOU MAY GRIEVE FOR THE PERFECT STATE THAT YOU FOUND THE BOOK IN. YOU MAY BEGIN TO SEE CREATIVE DESTRUCTION EVERYWHERE. YOU MAY BEGIN TO LIVE MORE RECKLESSLY.

DEAR READER/USER,

THIS VERSION OF <u>WRECK THIS JOURNAL</u>
WAS MADE TO BE USED WHILE YOU
ARE OUT IN THE WORLD. (HENCE
ITS PORTABLE SIZE).

IT HAS SOME NEW PROMPTS
SPECIFIC TO THE OUTDOORS
BUT ALSO CONTAINS SOME
OF YOUR OLD FAVORITES.
SO STOP READING THIS AND
GO OUTSIDE! TIME TO
START A NEW ADVENTURE.
HAPPY WRECKING.
SINCERELY YOURS,
KERI SMITH

INSTRUCTIONS

1. Carry this with you everywhere you go.
2. Follow the instructions on every page.
3. Order is not important.
4. Instructions are open to interpretation.
5. Experiment.

(work against your better judgment.)

materials

ideas
gum
glue
dirt
saliva
water
weather
garbage
plant life
pencil/pen
needle & thread
stamps
stickers
sticky things
sticks
spoons
comb
twist tie
ink
paint
grass
detergent
grease
tears
crayons

smells
hands
string
ball
unpredictability
spontaneity
photos
newspaper
white things
office supplies
wax
found items
stapler
food
tea/coffee
emotions
fears
shoes
matches
biology
scissors
tape
time
happenstance
gumption
sharp things

ADD YOUR OWN PAGE NUMBERS.

STARTING HERE

DEVISE A
WAY TO
CARRY
THE
JOURNAL
EVERYWHERE.

2

ACQUIRE A NAPKIN FROM
A RESTAURANT. WRITE
A SECRET ON IT.
GLUE IT HERE.

3

MAKE A MARK EVERY TIME YOU SPOT A BIRD.

4

Lick this page!

do not totch

CHOOSE YOUR OWN
WRECKING
METHOD

SIGN

19·12·2020

DATE

5

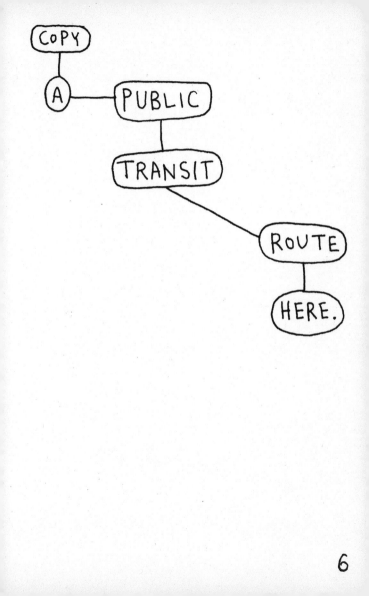

6

HIDE PARTS
OF THIS PAGE
ON YOUR
TRAVELS.

POKE HOLES IN
THIS PAGE USING
SOMETHING YOU FIND
ON YOUR TRAVELS.

8

FLOAT
THIS PAGE.

9

Put pencil marks
EVRYwhere

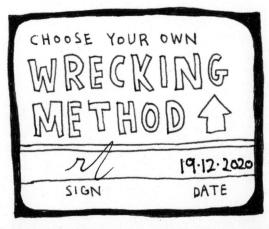

CHOOSE YOUR OWN

WRECKING
METHOD ⬆

SIGN   19·12·2020

DATE

USE THIS SPACE WHILE DREAMING OUTSIDE.

DRAW SOMETHING BASED ON THE

MOON

●	FULL	DRAW WHAT IS ABOVE YOU.
☾	WAXING	DRAW WHAT IS TO YOUR LEFT.
☽	WANING	DRAW WHAT IS TO YOUR RIGHT.

COVER THIS
PAGE WITH
ODD THINGS
YOU FIND.

14

DRAW
SOMETHING
HERE

←

WITH A PEN.
GO OUT IN THE
RAIN OR SNOW.
LET IT GET WET.

15

COLLECT NUMBERS
FROM THE WORLD HERE.

compost this page.

watch it deteriorate.

CHOOSE YOUR OWN
WRECKING
METHOD ⬆

SIGN   DATE

DOCUMENT TIME PASSING IN A NEW ENVIRONMENT.

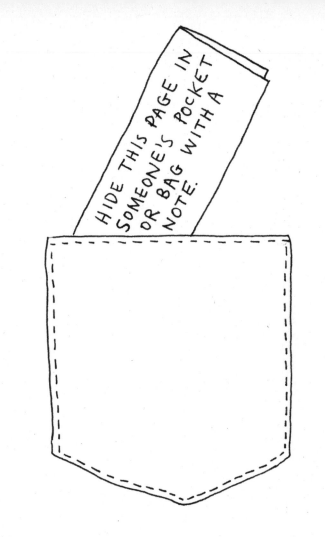

CLIMB UP HIGH

DROP THE JOURNAL.

WRITE LITTLE NOTES
To TEAR OUT AND LEAVE
FOR OTHERS (IN PUBLIC).

GO FOR A WALK, DRAG IT.

TIE A STRING TO THE JOURNAL.

GET THIS PAGE
STAMPED BY
SOMEONE.
(HINT: TRY THE POST
OFFICE.)

CHOOSE YOUR OWN

WRECKING
METHOD ⬆

_____

_____

SIGN   DATE

draw lines
ON THE BUS, ON A

While IN MOTION,
TRAIN, WHILE WALKING.

DROP MUD
HERE. REPEAT.

Infuse this
page with a
smell of your
choosing.

PLACE THIS PAGE
FACEDOWN ON
THE GROUND AND
KICK IT AROUND
FOR A WHILE.

CHOOSE YOUR OWN
WRECKING
METHOD ⬆

SIGN   DATE

COVER THIS PAGE

USING ONLY ITEMS FOUND IN THE OUTDOORS.

TRACE THINGS FROM OUTSIDE. LET THE LINES OVERLAP.

SMUSH
SOMETHING
COLORFUL
ONTO THIS
PAGE.

COVER THIS
PAGE IN LINES
THAT YOU FIND.

WHILE YOU ARE
OUT FOR A WALK,
SCRAPE THIS PAGE
ON A VARIETY
OF NATURAL
SURFACES AS
YOU GO.

CHOOSE YOUR OWN
WRECKING
METHOD ⬆

SIGN   DATE

COLLECT
DEAD
BUGS
HERE.

FILL THE ENTIRE PAGE WITH **WORDS** YOU SEE ON YOUR ADVENTURES.

TURN THIS PAGE BLACK*

*USING ITEMS FOUND IN THE WORLD.

THIS PAGE IS A
WORK IN PROGRESS.
(ADD SOMETHING
FROM EVERY
ENVIRONMENT YOU
VISIT IN A DAY.)

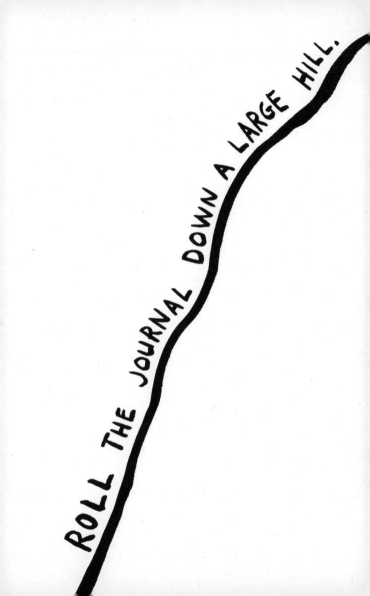

ROLL THE JOURNAL DOWN A LARGE HILL.

COVER THIS PAGE WITH <u>VERY TINY THOUGHTS</u>
FROM EVERYWHERE.

DO SOME LEAF PRINTS.

FIND A GREEN LEAF.
FIND A ROCK.
TURN PAGE OVER.
HAMMER THE SPOT
WHERE THE LEAF
IS USING THE ROCK.

FIND A WAY TO WEAR THE JOURNAL.

CHOOSE YOUR OWN

WRECKING
METHOD ⬆

SIGN   DATE

find
a
piece
of
string.

TIE THIS PAGE UP WITH IT.

TAKE A WALK.

THEN STAND HERE.

(WIPE YOUR FEET, JUMP UP AND DOWN.)

HANG THE JOURNAL IN A PUBLIC PLACE.
INVITE PEOPLE TO DRAW HERE.

USE THIS PLACE
FOR BLADES OF
GRASS YOU FIND.

COLLECT names, AUTOGRAPHS, OTHER PEOPLE'S DREAMS.

CHOOSE YOUR OWN

WRECKING METHOD ⬆

SIGN   DATE

WHILE WAITING FOR SOMETHING (FOOD, A PLANE, YOUR FRIEND TO ARRIVE), WRITE A LIST OF EVERYTHING YOU CAN SEE.

DIP THIS PAGE IN THREE DIFFERENT
SUBSTANCES FROM THREE DIFFERENT
ENVIRONMENTS

CUT OUT THESE BADGES.
LEAVE THEM IN A PUBLIC
PLACE FOR OTHER PEOPLE
TO WRECK.

THIS PAGE IS FOR HANDPRINTS
OR FINGERPRINTS.
GET THEM DIRTY THEN PRESS DOWN.

CHOOSE YOUR OWN

WRECKING
METHOD ⬆

SIGN   DATE

STAIN LOG

WRECKING LOCATION LOG

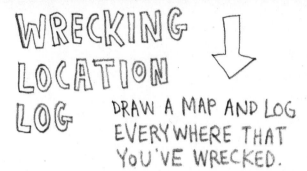

DRAW A MAP AND LOG
EVERYWHERE THAT
YOU'VE WRECKED.

ACKNOWLEDGMENTS

THIS BOOK WAS MADE WITH THE HELP OF THE FOLLOWING PEOPLE: JEFFERSON PITCHER, STEVE LAMBERT, CYNTHIA YARDLEY, MEG LEDER, FAITH HAMLIN, CORITA KENT, JOHN CAGE, ROSS MENDES, BRENDA UELAND, BRUNO MUNARI, CHARLES AND RAE EAMES, AND GEORGES PEREC. DEDICATED TO PERFECTIONISTS ALL OVER THE WORLD.

KERI SMITH IS AN AGENT FOR A SECRET UNDERGROUND ORGANIZATION WHOSE MISSION IS TO REANIMATE EVERYDAY LIFE AND QUESTION THE STATUS QUO. SHE SPENDS HER TIME CONDUCTING HER "RESEARCH" UP IN TREES WATCHING THE WORLD AND TAKING DETAILED NOTES. SHE USES HER FINDINGS TO CREATE BOOKS AND CONCEPTUAL ARTWORKS. YOU CAN FIND SOME OF HER RESEARCH AT KERISMITH.COM.

WHERE WILL YOU WRECK?
#WRECKEVERYWHERE

PENGUIN.COM/KERISMITH
KERISMITH.COM
KERISMITHBOOKS.TUMBLR.COM
TWITTER.COM/WRECKTHISTWIT

T401-0314